T0129860

HOW TO LIVE AN
Amazing Life

The no-nonsense guide to sorting your
life out and living the best life ever!

KAREN BEGGS

BALBOA.PRESS
A DIVISION OF HAY HOUSE

Balboa Press books may be ordered through booksellers or by contacting:

Balboa Press
A Division of Hay House
1663 Liberty Drive
Bloomington, IN 47403
www.balboapress.com
844-682-1282

Because of the dynamic nature of the Internet, any web addresses or links contained in this book may have changed since publication and may no longer be valid. The views expressed in this work are solely those of the author and do not necessarily reflect the views of the publisher, and the publisher hereby disclaims any responsibility for them.

The author of this book does not dispense medical advice or prescribe the use of any technique as a form of treatment for physical, emotional, or medical problems without the advice of a physician, either directly or indirectly. The intent of the author is only to offer information of a general nature to help you in your quest for emotional and spiritual well-being. In the event you use any of the information in this book for yourself, which is your constitutional right, the author and the publisher assume no responsibility for your actions.

Any people depicted in stock imagery provided by Getty Images are models, and such images are being used for illustrative purposes only.
Certain stock imagery © Getty Images.

Print information available on the last page.

ISBN: 979-8-7652-3388-7 (sc)
ISBN: 979-8-7652-3390-0 (hc)
ISBN: 979-8-7652-3389-4 (e)

Library of Congress Control Number: 2022917698

Balboa Press rev. date: 09/23/2022

HOW TO LIVE AN
Amazing Life

Easy ways to make small changes that
will impact your life enormously!

Contents

Acknowledgments

My Amazing book and Amazing life have been made so by the wonderful influence and friendships of truly Amazing people!

Firstly, to my parents, thank you for never putting any limits or boundaries onto anything we (me and Sis) ever did. You taught us to think bigger than ourselves, and to always respect and appreciate differences of opinions and people.

To my sister and best friends, thank you for your contagious positivity and can-do attitudes. You are Amazing and I luv yas!

To the Amazing guys I coach, your goals and the action you take inspire me daily. I love to be around you!

To my son Aadam, this is literally my only wish for you.

Karen xx

Lend me your ears and I'll change what you hear,
Lend me your eyes and I'll change what you see,
Lend me your hand and I'll change what you feel,
Lend me your mind and I'll change how you receive...

Moi

Welcome to My Introduction!

First, thank *you* for taking action and buying this book! I am really happy for you, as I genuinely believe that your life will improve if you take on board any one thing from this book. I'm writing this book because I love my life. I will share with you that my life wasn't always like this. I used to be like you. I was a weirdly quiet teenager and had a pretty interesting time during my twenties and It has literally taken me until my thirties to straighten everything out. I have spent over ten years reading every self-enhancement, self-motivation, and self-help book I could get my hands on, and not because I was desperate or weak, but because I wanted to know how to be the best version of me that I could be. I saw people living the life I wanted to be living and I wanted to find out how. I have transformed my own life, and live a life today that, ten years ago, I was dreaming about. I have had to deal with some serious amounts of crap in between, but I believe that it is how we deal with these life experiences that truly distinguishes winners from those who merely accept the shit. There are so many things we can do to help ourselves—tools we can use and small habits we can change that will create the most everlasting and huge changes with what can be quite a minimal effort initially. Reading other motivational books made me feel that some were too scientific and hard for me to read and digest, as the authors tried to prove their theories were real, while others were so cheesy I could sniff the cheese miles away. I wanted to write a book that was written as though a group of my friends were sitting around talking about this over lattes, wine, or whatever. I hope you find my tone refreshing and easy to understand.

Each chapter will introduce a way that you can make a small change in your routine or personal habits. I will explain a bit of theory, and then suggest easy ways you can implement that theory or perhaps provide examples of how I have done so in my own life. Each chapter will finish with an exercise for you to complete. Please don't think you will read the whole book and then come back to the exercises; you are human, busy, and probably won't. So please grab a pen and do the exercises as you go along. Your instinctive response is always best, and mostly true. Sometimes when we think too hard about things, our minds make us write what we think we should write. If you are having to think too hard about your answer, you're not doing it right. Just let your mental juices flow and accept the first answer that comes to your mind. By the end of this book, I want you to have actually feel as though you have made some progress in your life. I want to make an impact on your life today. I hope you will let me. Now, go! Get a pen! Get reading and get changing, progressing, learning, and succeeding!

To me (and Tony Robbins), *success* means that you are doing exactly what you want, with whom you want, where you want, how you want, and as much as you want. Not everyone wants the same things, so I have kept it pretty general so you can fill in your own blanks as you are thinking through the book. That's right: thinking is essential. Engage with me and I will help you engage with yourself and your life. How can you go and get this stuff that you want if you don't even know exactly what that is yet?

I welcome you to a journey of self-discovery and discovering your Amazingness! ☺

The One-Degree Theory

Think about what your life is going to look like if you keep doing what you're doing. Let's look at what your life could look like if you just changed a few simple things with a few baby steps.

The one-degree theory is so simple you are going to kick yourself in the leg for not having thought of it first! One of my (many) revelations from reading some (not all) motivational literature is that self-help gurus often claim you should change your life completely. You should change everything about yourself; you should say goodbye to your lazy old self and embrace your shiny new self. Well, this is fine if you have the willpower of a dynamo, but this, quite frankly, sounds like a shitload of work. And what if you are currently like I was? Your life is not a total fuck up. You are not homeless; you are not bankrupt (this doesn't mean that you are a millionaire either). What if you are a different type of person than some books seem to aim toward? Perhaps areas of your life just need tweaking with small changes and small steps. Perhaps there are areas in your life that need more help than others. A simple way to evaluate your needs is to write down each area of your life and mark each one out of ten, one being nonexistent or totally shit, and ten being so fabulous you could nearly pee a little bit at the excitement and thought of it.

The one-degree theory shows us that, over time, if we change even one area of our lives the smallest amount, we will end up in a very different position than where we started. Imagine you are traveling. You start off at point A, and you travel in a set direction. Now imagine you could go back to point A and change your direction one degree. Being ten thousand miles away is the difference between being in the Bahamas or being in Alaska. The point? I hope you'll freaking get it. The small shit creates the big shit.

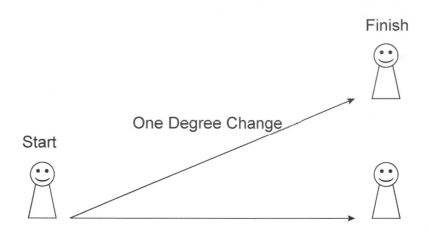

For example, if you have never worked out a day in your whole life, going to the gym and busting your balls every day for an hour would be hard to stick to. Instead, just aim to go for a thirty-minute walk twice per week. Sounds simple, right? It is, and by the end of the year you would have racked up fifty-two hours' worth of exercise that you normally wouldn't have done. This is a super example of little shit creating big shit.

Another example might be if you wanted to write a book (ahem!). This might seem like a daunting task—how could you ever write a whole book? But what if you only had to write one sentence per day? That might take ten seconds, and what happens when you sit down to write your one sentence? The ideas flow, and before you know it you've written a few paragraphs and you can now slouch off and have a hot bath and a glass of red! (That's where I'm off to now...ciao!)

Exercise

Answer the following questions from the perspective that if you do not change a thing, you will continue exactly as you are. And please don't be part of the ostrich syndrome movement, remove your head from the sand, look around, and answer honestly.

1. Who is in your life?
2. What is your relationship with them?
3. What is the style of your life? Are you a traveler? Are you a home bird?
4. What are your health and fitness levels like?
5. What about the material things in your life? What car do you drive? What is your house like?
6. What makes you really happy in this life?
7. What really frustrates you in this life?

Now answer the same questions again, this time from the perspective that you have made some small improvements in your life and your life has become what you really want it to look like.

1. Who is in your life?
2. What is your relationship with them?
3. What is the style of your life? Are you a traveler? Are you a home bird?
4. What are your health and fitness levels like?
5. What about the material things in your life? What car do you drive? What is your house like?
6. What makes you really happy in this life?
7. What really frustrates you in this life?

We don't need to wait to make small improvements to our environments.

The Power You Get from Having Standards

A sense of power is a great, resourceful mental state that you should be able to access whenever you need it. Having and feeling power allows you to have control over your emotional state, and therefore your mental stability and general well-being. If you're a lady (or just a well-developed human), life might seem like one big emotional fluctuation. So will you always be able to feel powerful? If you're a human, the answer is "probably not"; at several stages in your life, you will probably feel nervous, irritated, angry, or upset. What is important is your ability to then access the feeling of power. What I mean is this: how long will you allow yourself to suffer in a state of nervousness, irritation, or anger? The faster you can access your powerful state, the better life will be for you.

Regarding standards: let's get some. Having standards is a surefire way to ensure you have access to your most powerful state and self. Know what you want in and from your life. Know what you value. Know what you care about and know what you don't. Do not settle for second best, or that is what you will always get and end up tolerating. Learn to say no to second best, then visualize and take action toward first best, the bestest, and be grateful—genuinely grateful—when you receive it. You're in a restaurant and your friend or partner asks you what you want to eat, and you respond with, "I don't mind; what would you like?" Tell yourself off immediately, grab yourself by the balls, and decide what you would like to eat. Take a second and decide what you really want. Taste it, enjoy it, and be grateful you got it.

Getting standards can be difficult, so start small. Challenge yourself to have an opinion. Look around the room in which you are sitting. Do you like it? More specifically, do you like the chair you're sitting in? Yes or no? Don't say "maybe" or "it's all right" or "I don't really care," as this means you are accepting second best. You are accepting something you don't love and adore. You deserve to love and adore everything that your butt cheeks adorn. So tell me, do you love and adore the chair you are sitting on? Yes or no? Excellent! Practice this a lot. You don't have to say it out loud, but to become decisive you must question everything. In your head, ask always, *Is this acceptable to me or not? Ideally, how would I have it?* If you are feeling frustrated with something in life now, tell me what it is. Say it, even if it's in your head. What frustrates you? Now ask yourself honestly if it is your fault that you have ended up in this situation. If you are with a partner who is not right, are you there because you decided not to leave? Sometimes we fail to make a decision at all; you decided not to make that decision. And by deciding not to make that decision, you have unfortunately accepted a decision made by something else—fate perhaps, or another person. Are you in the wrong job? Why are *you* still in it? Have *you* decided not to spend an hour every evening applying for other jobs? Are *you* unhappy with your weight? Did you decide not to use that gym membership you purchased? Did *you* decide to eat the whole packet of biscuits? Yes, I think you did. I've been there and got the whole-packet-eating T-shirt. These revelations might be tough pills to swallow. If you are still reading this, it means you didn't throw the book out the window, but it also means you have resilience and are open to a little introspection, which will help us all out greatly in life. The following exercise will be difficult for you unless you throw your ego (get over it, of course we all have one!) out of the window immediately.

Ask this question of each area of your life: *is it perfect?* If you're the kind of person currently saying in your head, *Nothing's perfect*, then (a) I feel very sorry for you, and (b) just replace the word *perfect* with *as awesome as I in my wildest dreams would wish it to be*. If the area in your life is not perfect, then ask what it is that's not perfect about it. Identify what needs to change. Then write down what you have to do to make that area of your life perfect.

Exercise

Area	Identified Issue	Solution
Health		
Wealth/Finances		
Love		
Relationships		
Personal Development		
Fitness		
Work/Career		
Other		

Being Limitless

Remember the movie *Limitless* from years ago? It is awesome. If you haven't seen it, put it on your to-do list. The premise of the movie in a nutshell is this: what if you could take a pill and literally become limitless in terms of your capacity for life? The movie is very dramatic, and there's plenty of action, but seriously, think about this question for one quick second. What if you had no limits? What could you do? What if there was no one (not yourself or those other arrogant wankers) telling you what your limits are? If the world was your oyster, what would you do with it? I remember graduating, and everyone at that time telling me, "The world is now your oyster, go do whatever you want, do whatever it is that makes you happy"—essentially that my life was limitless. However, inside my head, I already thought I knew what I had to do. University equals debt for so many people. I had three jobs during university and still came out owing the government a fortune. So, in my head, I had already placed limits on myself in thinking that I had to get a job, I had to earn a salary, and get this debt repaid.

> A tablet a day and what I could do with my day was limitless.
> (*Limitless*)

Find your tablet. Find things that motivate you. Become limitless. Stop fucking about, making excuses or worse, and (even I have to kick my own ass for this sometimes) allowing others to make excuses for you.

Never regret time that you have spent doing other things. I turned forty this year and knew I wanted to be an entrepreneur from twenty years of age. I cannot regret that it took me eleven years to start businesses, as I have really been working out what the hell it was that I wanted to do and learning a lot by working for other people. I have maxed the experience by working for global, multinational companies, as well as for small independents in order to gather all the information that I can. Even if your past experience was all a bit crappy, at least you might now know what you don't want.

Identify it

Just notice when you place limits upon yourself, and make a personal commitment to acknowledging this and reforming the sentence in your head.

"I could never do that."

> *becomes*

"I have made the choice not to do that. If I really wanted to do it, I could work it out."

Exercise

Notice when you place limits on yourself. Notice how you say it in your head. Maybe it's not even a full sentence; maybe it's a snort when someone else pays you a compliment. Write down the sentence and then reconstruct the sentence the way that the shiny new you would tell you to.

What's your sentence?

Example 1

"I would never go traveling by myself."

becomes

"I can go traveling by myself; to be comfortable, I would need a clear plan and perhaps to visit people I know."

Example 2

"It's the wrong time to set up a business. It's a recession, I would really struggle."

becomes

"First, I'm already smart enough to understand that there are challenges to running a business. Second, I am passionate, and if I really wanted to, I could create a business plan that would survive and excel in this market."

Small Steps

In the book *The Secret*, Jack Canfield explains his theory on getting from A to B in terms of driving a car at night. Driving from Chicago to Los Angeles, the driver can only see 200 yards in front of the car, but keeps trooping and makes it across the country to Los Angeles. In lucky cases, all you will have to do is start the car going and you will eventually make it to your destination!

Two small tips are coming up. The first is not to sweat the small stuff (the stuff that's not really important), and the second is to still make the small things count. Allow yourself to let go of the small, crappy, insignificant things that put you in a bad mood. But do not allow yourself to accept crap, and make it known to others that you have higher standards.

Want to interact more with others? Enhance or fix your relationships with others? One small thing that you can do is to make a cup of tea for someone in your office. That person will be touched, he or she will smile at you, and you will feel good—everyone's a winner.

All of these ideas are ways to take small steps in your life. All of our small steps lead to bigger steps, which lead us to huge leaps. Before you know it, your life will look completely different from where you began.

Choose to start with something small so you can see how a little effort can create a little change. "I want massive change," I hear you cry. Well, get your butt into gear and create some massive action.

You will need to start small to prove change works, even if just to prove to yourself that you are capable of change. When you know this works, you will need to continue to pick bigger goals. Keep increasing the pressure and be confident that you will respond in the way that you should, and that will help you to achieve. When this happens, your confidence will increase and there will be nothing that you can't achieve. This is my disclaimer. Tony Robbins tells us this will lead to a huge impact on your life—if you are ready for huge action. If not, that is up to you. You are the expert of you. No one can tell you what you should do.

You know what they say? The only difference between ordinary and extraordinary is that little bit of extra. Get on it, and do something extra today.

Exercise

Choose one thing, big or small—your choice—that would make you a little different, or a little better, by doing it. When you choose it, break it down into *baby steps*, then *commit!* Then plan it into your diary and reward yourself for every step you take.

Exercise

Below, fill in five small, cost-effective things someone could do to make you smile.

Number	Lovely thing I would love someone to do for me
Example	*Give me a compliment.*
1	
2	
3	
4	
5	

Task

Do one of these things today and see how it feels. If it feels good, plan it in for tomorrow. If it doesn't feel good, you should readdress the thing you did today and perhaps ask another human being for some feedback, then take it on the chin like the champ you are.

The *E* Word

We all make them. We all know what this word is deep down, but we are reluctant to say it: *excuses*.

We all have them and make them all the time. In work, you make excuses for why you didn't finish the project on time. With your family, you make excuses for why you can't spend more time with them. With your friends, you make excuses for why you didn't make it to this event or that gathering. With your health, you make excuses that you don't have time, or that you're hungry now.

And worst of all?

Worst of all is the crap we tell ourselves, so let's stop it! Stop making excuses. Stop putting your life off.

Visualization—Be a Visionary and Live the Fantasy

The first time I heard of visualization was when I read *The Secret*. It was only then that I realized I had been doing this my whole life. If you have read *The Secret*, you will know what I am talking about. If not, (a) you should, and (b) the whole theory presupposes that, in essence, what you think about, you bring about in your life; you can attract whatever you need or want through the power of intention (intention being purposeful thought). I had been doing this my whole life. I was a big daydreamer at school, but when I worried about bills, they would seem to get worse; when I panicked about a social situation, I would somehow embarrass myself (plenty of stories here, but that's another book). On the other hand, if someone told me to cheer up and I actually tried, chances were good I would definitely feel slightly cheered. If someone said, "Things will work out okay" and I believed that person, then they always did.

If you prefer to watch a movie, there is a film version of *The Secret* that tells you (you as a kid) to imagine a bike, and the next day your granddad will arrive at your door with the bike. When you first hear this concept—that you can attract anything you want by whizzing a thought through your mind—you will probably think,

Yeah right, pull the other one! I know I did! How could that possibly be right? I can only really explain it like this: life is not a set thing that we all experience and perceive to be, but rather life is how we are trained or we choose to perceive it to be. Literally, whether you think the glass is half full or half empty, you will be right. My sister and I grew up in exactly the same environment, with the same beliefs and morals, and yet our personalities, perceptions, and therefore experience of life is entirely different. I personally would rather make the choice to spend my time here, perceiving life to be lovely, fluffy, and pink rather than grey, bitter, and tough. I now *know* that this works for me in my life. This is not me trying to pull a fast one on you—this is actually real. I have too many examples of when the law of attraction has worked in my life to ignore it.

Visualization is the key to the law of attraction. Bob Proctor says, "If you can see it in your mind, you will hold it in your hand." You will find it impossible to reach your dreams if you don't know what they are or cannot imagine in your mind how they look, feel, sound, and smell. Check through magazines, books, and internet sites, and dream big. Do not be afraid to dream big. If you dream of a fifteen-bedroom mansion and someday end up living in a twelve-bedroom mansion, would you be terribly disappointed? I don't think so.

Separate your life into whatever sections you think are relevant: health and fitness, finances, relationships, career, personal development, social satisfaction—whatever you want. Categorize these sections and get your ideal vision of what your life looks like. Buy yourself a notebook, use your laptop and open a folder whatever works and start collecting your visions. Jack Canfield talks about a goals book where you can title the top of each page with your goal and make the pictures relevant depending on what you want to achieve, whether it is a lifestyle you visualize or a goal you wish to achieve. (For a good example of a vision board, check out my Facebook page. I have my personal vision board on it. www.facebook.com/howtoliveanamazinglife.)

While it is certainly more important and pleasant to visualize what you do want, establishing this clearly might occasionally come from having a very clear picture of what you do not want. For example, if you are imagining your ideal partner, you might find yourself saying things like, "I don't mind what he or she looks like" or "I don't mind whatever habits he or she has." This is not very specific. You need to be clear. Make a list of traits you do not want your partner to have, then turn each into a positive trait. For example, if you are a lovely lady reading my book, while you are visualizing the man (or lady) of your dreams you might initially be tempted to say something like "I don't want a man with a temper." You can easily modify this to become "I want a man who is calm, cool, and collected." Your wish list points do not need to be deal breakers, but rather preferences that help you imagine what this person will potentially look like, be like, and smell like.

Another example might be when I need to lose a couple of pounds. I visualize how energetic and sexy I will feel, how trim and svelte I will look in a new dress I am going to buy. But sometimes it can be equally (if not more) motivating to think about the negative consequences of not losing weight. You need to get yourself to a point where you can say "That is it" or "I'm sick of this" or "Enough is enough! If I do not lose weight, I will continue to feel lethargic and sleepy. I will feel frumpy. I won't even be able to wear certain trousers anymore, and I definitely won't be feeling too sexy! If I don't lose weight, my son will grow up with an unfit mother, and they will even adopt the same eating behaviors that I have." These negative thoughts can sometimes be even more motivating than the positive ones, so we should all use both sides as motivators. If we're talking about more than a few kilos, think of the health complications you will be more likely to have, or think of the health benefits you will see. If you have family or a partner, think of the difference it will make in their lives. Ask yourself, *What is carrying the extra weight holding me back from? What do I wish I could do but can't because I am overweight?* Motivating yourself from both the good and the bad side at the same time will help you get there faster.

If there is something you want, get a picture of it. Dream about it, think about how you will feel when you have it, think about how people will react to you when you have it—just let yourself enjoy dreaming about it. Be as specific as possible: choose the color, shape, size, and make of anything you want, whether it is a car or a partner. Be specific. Specific visions produce specific resultsStill considering it? Start off with visualizing your day ahead. Before you get out of bed in the morning, keep your eyes closed and just imagine how your day is going to be. Say this: *I'm in the shower. It's hot and refreshing. I'm ready and heading to work The roads are clear. I have a wonderfully positive and productive meeting with my boss at nine am. I eat a yummy salad for lunch and I feel so healthy, I have a really productive afternoon and I come home and enjoy quality time with my family, flatmate, or myself.* You will see that by telling your mind how your day will look, more often than not your day will go exactly as (or at least close to how) you imagined that morning in the shower.

Another great visualization tool I have recently used is to write your personal biography as it would look if your life was perfect. Here's a sample of what mine will look like in the future, considering I'm currently writing this book.

Biography

I am a published author. I have a range of books and coaching based products for sale and have found reliable distributors all over the world. I am an accredited coach and NLP practitioner. I have the most amazing coaching clients, with most of my work getting done online. My finances are secure and I am able to work for myself, with my own schedule. Frequently, I am asked to do a motivational talk, either at a large corporation or at a motivational event. I love doing these, as the energy is awesome. I am in talks with some very influential people, taking my book, show, and courses farther, wider, and bigger.

Your turn

Write yours here. Write as though you have it already. Use present tense and not future, otherwise you will be indirectly visualizing where the vision will stay: in the future.

Decide your vision, see your vision, live your vision and be a visionary.

Exercise

Link this with the lists you have written previously. Can you find pictures that symbolize what you want to do? Scrapbook or create a folder on your laptop, iPad, or other device, and Google the images of the life and lifestyle you want. Save the pictures for you to see anytime you want. The easiest way to visualize is to watch your slideshow during some of your me time. Talk about multitasking!

Fake it until You Make it

I bet that you have heard of this one: "Fake it until you make it." This means visualizing what you want to be like or have in life and acting as though you already have it. Now, I am not totally encouraging you to make up lies about your life, or about your brand new helicopter, and gosh, how will you park it on the roof tonight? But I am talking about little things. For example, maybe you wish you were more confident, but you normally tell people that you really lack confidence, or you hate talking in front of people, or make some other statement that indicates you are not the most confident person in the world. When you think this and when you say it out loud, you make it stronger. You make it real, and you actually make yourself lack confidence even more. Try turning this around slightly. If you can't bring yourself to say "I am very confident," then try saying "I am more confident than I used to be" or try saying "I think I am getting more confident as I get older." What you say and what you think will eventually become exactly what you are. You will gradually become more confident, because as you say it, and say it out loud, you make it stronger, you make it real, and you create a more confident you every time you say it.

"Oh, bite my Cadbury's Flake and you will be sooooo silky and soooo smooooooth and so delicious to all men, they will be drooling over you, while you stuff your chubby cheeks with a chocolate stick." Well they wouldn't say that on advertisements, would they?

Advertising works. That's why companies spend millions on elaborate campaigns. The returns are sometimes thousands of times more than what they put in. Advertise your goals to yourself. Paint a picture of how you will feel and look and appear to others. What will they say about you? What will they feel towards you?

Think of faking it as marketing yourself. I come from a sales and marketing background, so this makes total sense to me. A brand becomes what we market it as—literally what we say it is. Volvo became the safest family car because Volvo told us it was. Of course they have data to support this, but they didn't promote themselves as the sexiest car, or the fastest car. They wanted to be the chosen, safe family car. Diesel is trendy and exclusive because they tell us it is. Chanel is feminine and classic because the branding tells us it is. You decide what your brand is, and you tell everyone what it is.

Task

Write your own mantras. See super tips below.

Exercise

Writing your goals can be tricky and, as we've talked about, our language plays a bigger part in our success than we ever knew before.

In the Positive

When writing your goals down, you must create the list in the positive. For example, don't write "I have a more supportive family" as this still alludes to the fact that, deep down, you don't think you have. Get specific. You should write, "My family supports me with every decision I make, and their support enlightens and strengthens." Another mantra you might write could be "I don't smoke anymore." This alludes to the fact that you did smoke and, whether you smoke or not, makes you think about smoking. What you could write instead is, "Every breath I take is clean and supports my body by healing, oxygenating, and energizing."

In the Present

Life is a gift, in the present; it is literally a present for you, right now. Are you curious, opening it like the gift it is, or are you cautiously peeking inside and sniffing to check it's not a pile of the brown stuff?

Write your goal as if you have already reached it. Do not write "Someday I will drive a Mercedes" as someday you might, but it definitely won't be today. Write instead "I drive a gorgeous SLK Mercedes, it's silver, and the seats inside are tan leather." The facts show us that people who set goals, specific goals, are much more likely to achieve them.

Stuck for ideas?

I am beautiful today and every day.

My family adores and supports me.

My children are happy and healthy, and growing in every way I had hoped.

My career is blossoming, and every day I am presented with new challenges that stimulate me.

I can achieve anything I want to.

I am attractive to all and am attracting awesome friends into my life all of the time.

I love my house, my garden, my…

I learn and feel like I'm personally developing all of the time.

I am fit and healthy and progressing with this every week.

I live the life that I dreamed of, a life of luxury, and I am able to afford everything I need and desire.

I am a successful writer and speaker, and travel the world doing what I love.

Ask! The Most Important Question!

"If you don't ask, you don't get!" Do you remember this one? My mum used to say this to me a lot. I never realized how important this was. So far, we have done a lot of work establishing what it is we actually want out of life (goal setting) and assessing why it is so important to us (motivation). So why would we struggle on by ourselves and never ask anyone for help? If we are starting a business, why are we too shy to ask anyone to buy our product or service, or ask anyone to refer us to the people and customers we need?

Nowadays (Granddad's favorite word right there), there are so many easy ways to get in touch with new people. Social media has opened up a world of people to us that we never had access to before. In business, I regularly use LinkedIn to contact people I need for my business. If someone writes to me on any social media site and tells me why he or she wants to be put in contact with someone else, I definitely help that person. Use technology, embrace technology, and if you don't know how to use it, ask someone who does know for a tutorial. Buy someone a coffee and get this free information. It will literally change your life. Search and you will find. Ask and you shall receive. Fact.

Asking is indeed a skill. Brilliant salespeople never have to use pressure to sell anything—they will only ask questions. Brilliant coaches will ask questions to help you reach a moment of clarity, or to help you explore all possibilities as to why you're being coached. But it is not their place to tell you anything. Brilliant managers will communicate with you fantastically, and what will they do? They will ask questions, ask your opinion, listen to you, and only then, advise you, mentor you rather than dictate to you. Asking questions is a life skill, so get on it and learn how to develop it. This skill will even help you with your family. Imagine being able to coach them into doing what you want without even asking. Imagine the power you would have. If you're scared of rejection, learn to accept that rejection will be an inevitable part of this question-asking experience. Learn to accept rejection as feedback for how you asked the question. Make yourself ask the question in a different way the next time so you get a different result. Ask the question as if the other person has already said yes, as if you're happy because you have gotten exactly what you want. Imagine yourself in that already-have-what-you-want place, and ask, ask, and ask again.

Exercise

Which questions do you need to ask to reach the next level? Whom do you need to ask? When do you need to ask? Create a ticklist and put it into your diary so you can celebrate when you have done it.

Example

	Question	Who?	When?	Done?
Karen's example	What contacts do I have to help me promote my books and services?	My publisher	This week!	√
Q1				
Q3				
Q3				
Q4				
Q5				

Watch Your Language, Bitch!

I completed a degree in English Literature and the difference between positive and negative connotations in language is so simple and yet the effect is massive. If you know some literature, you will know well the difference in tone and feeling between Sylvia Plath and Tony Robbins. We have spoken about decisions and how becoming decisive will help your language. What's the difference between "I don't mind it" and "I love it"? These two statements are entirely different. What's the difference between someone who says "I can't," "I won't," "I hope," or "I'll try" and the person who says "I can," "I will," "I know," or "I'm doing"? I will tell you the difference: the second person has the mindset of a winner. The first person might be a lovely individual, but he or she cannot be incredibly successful because successful people talk like winners. They can, they know, and they do, and they will continue to do so.

The difference here is in the decision you make: to grin and bear something you don't particularly want to do, or to choose something you adore and love. What's the difference between "I hope I can change" and "I know I can change—I already have"? Again, it is a really small difference, and that is being affirmative. Know who you are. Know what you expect. Know your standards. Know when to say yes, and when to say no. I guarantee you will be at least ten times happier and more confident in yourself than you currently are.

Say "No Thanks" to Martyrdom

Trust me, no one will thank you for being a martyr. They rarely do, especially not if you are whining the whole time you are doing it. If deep down you already know you're a martyr, then please stop. Thank you! Do exactly what you want to do, do what you are capable of doing, and do what will make you feel good because you feel you should. Do not do what you don't want to do—you will eventually begrudge it. Do not offer to do what you're not capable of doing—you will eventually resent it. Do not do what will make you feel bad—do I even have to tell you why not for this one? How many times have you said yes when all you really wanted to say was no? Life is too short. You are in control of your life, control of your destiny, and control of your happiness. Ask yourself, "Is this fun? Do I want to be here? Am I loving this right now?" Is the answer no? Then you need to make a decision: how much do you need to be here, and what can you do to prevent yourself from getting in this situation in the future? Only you know. I cannot tell you, and neither can anyone else, although you probably know several people who will tell you they can—they're wrong, and in fact are not very good friends to be telling you what to do. Lose them, because they are losers. Surround yourself with people who love you, appreciate you, and care about you, people who you see make an effort to love you and look after you. If you think they love you and they treat you like shit, and then even try to tell you it's for your own good, lose them because they're losers.

Don't be a martyr. Get in control of your life!

Me Time

Nourish yourself first so that you can nourish others.

You will have seen human examples of the martyr type: they are so lovely, and you witness them running around trying to do as much as they can for everyone else. They are smiling, laughing, and making jokes, but there is sadness in the depth of their eyes. They seem like the nicest people in the world, but really we all know they are dying a little bit on the inside because they haven't had a minute to themselves in ages. Haven't we all seen someone like this? Don't you know someone who is like this? In fact, think hard—is it you? This selflessness is a beautiful quality in a fellow human being, but to look after others you must look after number one, and that is (drum roll please) you. *Respect* yourself enough (by enough read as much as everyone else) to look after and take care of yourself, and then let the kindness and goodness that you feel overflow into other aspects of the rest of your life. Cheesy, but true. If you are happy, those around you will be too.

Research confirms that if you are married or living with someone, you become completely susceptible to his or her emotional state. So that means twice the amount of bad moods that you would usually have, but also twice as many good moods as you would have. ☺ With that emotional rollercoaster, it is essential we look after ourselves first so we can look after others. On flight safety announcements, they tell you to put on your own oxygen masks on first before helping anyone else. You cannot physically help your child or partner or randomer sitting beside you if you have no oxygen yourself. This is simple, practical, and life preserving. Supply your own oxygen and then you can help everyone around you.

We are not animals, and what differentiates us is the fact that we are thinking, philosophical beings. We need time to process information, ideas and theories. We need time to reflect and dream, and denying ourselves this time will result in frustration. We owe it to ourselves and the people we choose to be around to give ourselves time to do this. Watching the latest Netflix series does not count. Watching television does not let you process information; you are numb to the world, but actually concentrating on whatever is on. Do something selfish for yourself: take a bath, go for a walk, go to the gym, lie down in a darkened room, take yourself out for a coffee (or vino). Bring to mind a free time during the day that you could use for yourself. If you can't think of a time, do you watch television? Yes? Then yes, you do have time. It's up to you what you choose to spend your time doing. Do I watch television? Yes, definitely. Do I watch television for three hours every day? No, I do not. I used to, but no more. Imagine that your day starts with you; you have one hour to do whatever you want. You can go to the gym, you can go for a walk, you can just sit and make yourself a cup of coffee while reading the paper (paper version or virtual). This may involve you waking up one hour earlier. Imagine what you will be like with others afterwards. Do you think you might be a nicer person to be around? I'm pretty sure you would be. Do you think and feel like you have more patience with others? I'm sure you will. Do you see yourself having more fun and hearing more laughter with your friends and family? I'm sure you will. So let's fully imagine together what your day would look like and sound like when you've had time for yourself. Can you picture it? Can you see your colleagues, friends, and family responding to you in a positive way? Imagine having that time. Now imagine your next interaction. Is it with a family member or a work colleague? How are you with them now? Do you look more relaxed? Do you sound friendlier, contented, and more patient? Are you more engaged with them, more so than normal? I guarantee that you are a nicer person in this vision. Please do yourself (and everyone else) a favor and love yourself. *Love yourself the way you want others to love you, and the way you want to love others.*

You know that old cheesy cracker: no one else will love you until you love yourself? Please get that it's a cliché for a reason. There is something to this.

However you want to spend your me time, just make sure you do it. Make sure you do it daily. *Allow* yourself the time to do this.

Total Time: What do you need today? Five to sixty minutes.

Exercise

Right now, let's write a list of ways you can have some me time. These will be different for everyone, so write your own. It's up to you if they cost a couple of dollars or are totally free.

Number	Ways to get me time
Example	i. Light some candles and go take a bath (lock the door!) ii. A 20-minute meditation iii. Get up early and go to the gym iv. Get up early, make yourself a coffee, and just breathe
1	
2	
3	
4	
5	

Task

Plan in me time today or tomorrow, depending on how hectic your life currently is, but definitely within this week. Take a mental note (and also fill it in below) of how you feel afterwards. Take note of how you treat those around you afterwards. Are you a nicer person? Is it *actually* a good thing for you and those around you if you take this time? Is it *actually* a good thing for your career and for your friends if you take this time? I hear you thinking yes. I know that you know you are worth it. You are a walking L'Oréal advert. Shout it loud, shout it proud—"I'm worth it!"

Date	Me time spent how?	How did I feel before?	How did I feel after?

Laugh

It is now scientifically proven that laughter heals the soul; it makes you feel better. You work tummy muscles (mental note: for abs, get laughing more, Karen!) and burn calories. It can change your posture, can change how others perceive your character and, most importantly, can and does change how good you feel about yourself. So our main purpose in life must be to find what makes us smile and laugh. Let's proactively search for it daily.

A good starting point is to always make sure you are the first person to laugh at yourself. Apart from making you a much more humble and approachable person, you are also laughing and humoring yourself. People like people who can laugh at themselves, and quite often this can dissolve an awkward situation. Go get ripping the piss out of yourself.

Are there certain people who make you smile and laugh? Search for ways to spend time with them (without looking like a complete stalker). Are there programs or comedians that make you laugh? If so, watch their shows when you have a bad day and you're feeling crap, because crap days do, in fact, happen to us all—to some more than others. What is important is what you do when you're in this crapzone to get yourself out of it as quickly as possible.

If you have ever been to a weight loss group, you know they tell you that preparation is the key to losing weight. Clear out the crap: get rid of the junk food from your cupboards to eliminate temptation. They will also tell you to have plenty of healthy snacks ready, because one thing is for sure in life: you will have an appetite and want to eat.

Well, you need to do the same sort of thing to ensure happiness in your life. Get rid of the stuff that really makes you unhappy. Life is full of ups and downs, not just with life events but with hormones as well, especially if you are female. You have so many hormones raging around your body that sometimes it feels impossible just to get through the day. Prepare for this and understand yourself. What triggers you? What really pisses you off? What brings you out of a bad mood? What flicks that switch? It is only when you know these things that you can have full control of yourself and your moods. Who says you have to be in that bad mood? What if you could pull yourself back at the click of your own magical, mood-changing fingers? How freaking cool would that be?

Exercise

List the things that make you smile. Then list the things that make you laugh. These can include people, things, funny situations, even memories. Stockpile these images, people, and things so you have your stash ready to go to when you need it. (Perhaps you won't even need it; you might just have a moment when you want to fill yourself up with something lovely.)

Things that make me smile
Example   Chatting with my best friend
1
2
3
4
5

Things that make me laugh out loud
Example   Current hilarious comedy show

1

2

3

4

5

Thank You

Gratitude is the key to getting more and more of everything you love and adore.

I hear what you're saying: "How the hell can I be grateful when the bills are pouring in through the front door and I can barely breathe?" While it's so important to deal with the reality of your situation, it is more important to be thankful for what you do have. People who say "thank you" are more grateful and happy than those who don't. Fit saying thank you into your daily life as much as possible. Say thank you to everyone who does anything for you during the day. A door held open, a cup of coffee made by a colleague, a kind word—these are all things to be grateful for.

Write down everything you are grateful for today. Keep going until you have nothing more to write. Pick this list up every day and add to it. As your gratitude list gets longer and longer you will realize all the good that you have in your life, and as you acknowledge it, it will expand throughout your life, creating more to be grateful for.

As you do find yourself in a position to pay off bills, say thank you. Say it out loud, and be happy that you can afford to pay something off; you will attract more of this to you.

Dig out your balance wheel and go through the sections of your life you identified as most important. Write a list of all the things you are grateful for: your health, your family, your friends, your career, job, or business, your finances, your self-development. See how the list of amazing things in your life just grows and grows?

Exercise

Health

Thank you for my perfect health and ever increasing fitness. Thank you for my energy and healthy body. Thank you for my ears to hear my favorite tunes. Thank you for my eyes so I can see the people I love and all the beauty around me in the world. Thank you for my mouth so I can taste yummy food. Thank you.

Work

I am so grateful for my salary. Thank you. I love when I get my paycheck. I am so grateful to have the opportunity to work with lovely people and experts, and I love my lovely clients. Thank you.

Family

Thank you for my family; they are the most important people to me. I love my parents, my sister is my best friend, my son inspires me and my family members are all young, healthy, and so cool. I love spending time with them, so thank you.

Friends

Thank you for my wonderful friends. I love the diversity and opinions they bring into my life. I'm so happy and grateful that I have friends to have coffee with, friends to go to the movies with, friends to go dancing with, and friends who open my eyes to new things all the time. Thank you.

Finances

Thank you so much for my current bank account. I have more money than I have ever had before, and my monthly salary and income streams grow and grow and grow. Thank you. Thank you for giving me *more* than enough money to pay each and every bill that arrives, and thank you for giving me enough to save, to invest, and to splurge. Thank you.

Professional Development

Thank you for the courage to write this book. I'm learning so much, and it is bringing new and amazing people into my life every day. Thank you. Thank you to my boss, who encouraged me to do a coaching course that our company runs, which led to another coaching with NLP course, which led to my awesome coaching clients. I feel like I get more from them than they do from me sometimes. Thank you.

Get Your Physical Body behind Your Mission

Imagine someone who is depressed. Look at how he holds his body. What kinds of words describe him? Slumped? Weighted? Worn down? Exactly. He feels and looks like a huge weight is bearing down on his shoulders. Everything on his face will be drooping: his eyebrows, the corners of his mouth; his eyes even look sad and depressed. His skin is colorless and lifeless, and he might actually look ill.

Now let's then look at someone who loves life. Imagine that person who loves his life feels passion for what he does and looks forward to waking up every single day. What does he look like? Exactly: the total opposite. He will look like his shoulders are held up by the strings of the angels of life that watch over him. He will look light as a feather, as if he glides through his day and glides through life. He looks excited, he sits upright, and he is completely engaged with life. Every feature in his face points to the sky; his eyebrows, his light-filled eyes, the corners of his eyes, because he is delighted to see you, to meet you, to greet you.

Exercise

Physically do this: sit slumped over with your sad, wrinkly face looking down. How do you feel? I will assume it's not freaking amazing, is it? Now take a deep breath inwards and, as you sit up straight, lift your eyebrows, smile, and look towards the sky. Do you feel a little bit different now?

In fact, I would go as far to say that it is pretty difficult to feel like shit in this upright position. Do you agree? Coordinate your physical body to adapt to your shiny new mindset. If you want to be positive and energetic and outgoing, you are going to have to change something physically. If you currently don't look after your body very well, perhaps you think you can continue to treat your body like shit and have it respond in some miraculous way? Unless you are twenty years old, I suggest you wake up and smell your dead, wasting body cells.

Get up, stand up, strut your funky stuff now.

You will feel better for it. You will have respect for what your body can do. You will love yourself even more than you do right now.

Don't feel like it? Whatever, loser. Reread the chapter about the *e* word.

You have no excuse. There are so many different and fun programs and exercises to try. Perhaps you just want to go for a walk now and again. Perhaps you need something very strict and structured to keep you going. Maybe paying for a gym will entice you to go, or having a personal trainer will get you started and help you get on track. Work out where you're excited or curious to try, and make a commitment to go just once.

Motion is part of the word EMotion.
Motion creates Emotions within you. Fact.

Exercise

What do you currently do?

What do you like doing?

What would make you fitter? How much fun would this be?

How much time can you fit into your normal day to get fitter? (If you say "none" to this, but watch any television ever, I will kick your butt.) Who can help you become fitter?

What can you do for free to become fitter?

Can you afford to spend any money on this area of your life?

Yes? How much?

When will you do it?

Reading, Learning, Developing

How many books have you read within the past six months? How many courses have you taken? How many seminars have you attended? If the answer is none, then ask yourself why not? What is stopping you from learning and growing? Information is all around us; it is literally at our fingertips. Stimulate yourself. Yes, you heard me right. You go to the gym, you work out, now try working out the most powerful muscle you have: your brain. You don't have to pay for expensive courses, as everything you need to know is quite freely available on the Internet. Explore it and see where it leads you.

I like to read about amazing people, motivational speakers and entrepreneurs who have done what I want to do, who have achieved what I want to achieve. Now I can't stop reading about them. This inspires me, it gives me energy, and for ten years was the reason I was able to get up in the morning and go to work for someone else whilst I absorbed and planned my own global domination! I am inspired by people who start with nothing and reach a point in their lives where they have everything they ever dreamed of. I am not just interested in millionaires, and don't get me wrong. While the dosh is important, true wealth, for me, is when you have all the happiness, love, and health that you need. These are the people I read about. If you think you are already smart enough, then sad for you, because you're an idiot. If you think there is nothing you can learn, then maybe you don't even deserve to move forward. If you think you know it all already, you are in for a big shock someday. To learn is to be humble. It is to accept that you do not know it all, that you can learn, that you can develop, that you can change. And change is the key to life. Remember that the only constant thing we can rely on in life is, in fact, change.

Passion—What's Yours?

What makes you feel alive? I really hope that you can find a way to find this in your life. Why? Why not pick the logical route that you don't really want to do? Well, the answer is simple: passion. If you want something badly enough, if you feel passionately about something, you will find a way to get it. You will not be put off by the first bump that appears in the road. Your mind will generate solutions before it even registers the bump as a problem. You will find energy for your project that you have never seen before. You will find people who can help you, and you won't even worry about sounding like a weirdo.

Find your passion and follow it, and success will follow you.

The Power of Music

You know that moment in the evening of a girls' night out when you think you're done and you're about to get a taxi to go home, and then... tuuuuuunnnnnne! That song comes on that makes the blood surge through your veins, makes you dance like you are Beyoncé herself. We all have those songs that we cannot stop ourselves from singing and dancing to. For me, music can literally change my mood within seconds. If I want to pause from writing because I feel sleepy or distracted, I start playing a music list, and within five seconds I feel totally rejuvenated. Find the tunes that make you move, that make you sing out loud, that make you smile or sit up straighter and tap your foot. Keep and use these songs as a tool to help rejuvenate your energy levels when you need to.

Exercise

Depending on how technologically advanced you are, set up an emergency folder in your music account. Think of songs that, no matter what mood you're in, will have you tapping your feet and singing along in no time. Everyone has these. Find yours.

Get That Friday Feeling

Okay, so I'm making you visualize, making you feel it. But are you *really*—and I mean *really*—feeling what it is like to have everything you want in life now? Fair enough, it's freaking hard. How could you possibly know what it feels like to have something that you don't have? However, that feeling of not having it, that gut wrenching emptiness of wanting something you don't have is really damaging. You need to replace it with the feeling that you are delighted to have it; here's how.

As a kid, I was obsessed with catalogs and the thoughts of getting more *stuff*. I used to go through the catalogs reading and feeling like (imaging) I was a millionaire and could order anything I wanted without worrying, or even thinking, about the dosh. I would see a dress I liked, and I would tell my imaginary personal shopper that I would take it in red, blue, beige and, oh, I like the burgundy as well, please. I had such a great imagination and I was so generous to myself (and I used to pretend order presents for others too!). I felt what it really would feel like to be in that situation, without a care in the world, ordering whatever I wanted to order, whenever I wanted to order it. Without knowing it, I was visualizing what it would feel like to be financially independent. It felt good. I was carefree and relaxed. I wasn't worried about spending, or about the credit card being rejected, or about the statement coming in at the end of the month. I was free and could see and order whatever and whenever I wanted, and I was excited.

This is the state you need to be in to become truly motivated to achieve your goals and success. What will make you get out of bed earlier every morning and hit the gym? Perhaps a picture stuck to your fridge will do it for a while. Maybe a personal trainer will work for you while you can be bothered to meet up with him/her. Perhaps a guilt trip from your family and friends will also help for a while. But what will motivate you forever is not only *wanting* to do something, but feeling like you really *need* to do it. When you can feel it, you will believe you can have it, and *then*…then you will *need* to get it. This *need* is indeed that same Friday feeling.

Assess and Evaluate

Measuring and Success: Knowing your Enemy

For all of us, we must appreciate what we have done up to this point. What *you* have done so far has brought you here, to be reading, learning, and developing. Assess your current life situation; visually take a picture of where you are today and compare it with a picture of where you want to be, and evaluate ways you could get there. It's amazing when you take a moment to objectively look at where you are and establish where you want to be; your brain automatically starts creating ways you could do it.

Get into the habit of asking yourself and others to rate things. I rate things out of ten, but maybe you want to rate things by colors or feelings. I know a family who doesn't do anything that doesn't feel awesome. Ask your partner how he or she rates your relationship. If you're surprised by the answer, you probably need to work on your communication. What if you asked your boss how he or she rates your performance. Have you ever done this? Well, strap on a pair, ask the tough questions, and hopefully get some useful feedback. If you're trying to start your own business, be brutal with yourself. Be engaged and passionate about what you do, but not so engaged that you are blinkered and can't see the bigger picture. (The bigger picture, by the way, is *not* you— it's your customer. Ask your customer to rate your product and note that rating is important. Don't ask them if they like it, as the majority of people will say yes to pacify you. This is *not* useful. Ask them to rate, then take the feedback and act upon what bothers or inspires you). Ask your children to rate your parenting skills. I know this one sounds instinctively reverse, but it is an important relationship that we must work on, and hopefully you think you have something to learn in all areas of your life. Once you receive a rating, don't forget to ask the most important question "what can I do improve? What can I do to make it a ten? What can I do to make this *awesome*?"

Let me introduce you to the wheel of life. The purpose of this is to establish how you feel about various aspects of your life. The aim is to head towards achieving a balance: if you are incredibly rich but have no friends, no loved ones, no satisfaction with your personal development, then how happy are you? True wealth and happiness means having abundance and happiness in all of these areas, and you can only work on an area once you establish which one needs attention. I have given you two wheels here: one for you to complete at the beginning of this book and one to come back to afterwards (I will remind you, of course) to see if this book has helped you move on in certain areas of your life. I do hope so. And please, get in contact with me and let me know if you see a difference.

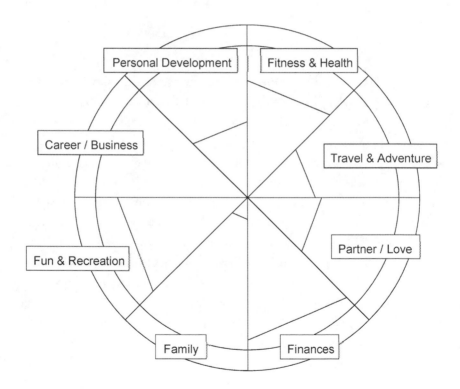

Imagine if this was your wheel of life. Look at this for a bumpy ride. This is not wealth and abundance; this is imbalance, and will affect the other areas of your life.

In life, every decision is your choice. For every situation, conversation, or decision, you have the power. You have the choice. You can make an awesome choice or a shit choice. (If you make no choice, this counts as a shit one, by the way!). Unfortunately, we limit ourselves all the time. It is your choice if you completely transform your life or situation, and it is your choice if you simply work on key areas that annoy you the most. Essentially, we are all aiming for that wonderfully sweet, smooth ride! ;)

If you have seen this tool before, apologies for boring you, but it's a great tool to revisit and see how your life cycle is changing or improving. If you have not seen this before, it is a great tool that will give you loads of clarity about what's going on in your life. Let's take this one step further and color each section. Color helps our brains process information, and we automatically associate colors with real emotions and feelings. For me, family is pink, as pink represents love; work is blue, as blue represents stability; and perhaps green for health. Choose your own colors and trust me, the more you embrace this, the more you will get out of it.

Now let's take your discoveries further. Imagine you are going to color each of your sections fully. What would it take to make each section a ten? If you say it's a six, then you feel that something is missing or not working, so you need to say it out loud. Use shorthand or codes that you will understand if you worry about someone else reading this. When you do this, within five minutes you will have established your current situation and what you need to fix or achieve to make it a ten. Let's understand that the only thing constant in life is change, so not all sections will be a full ten at the same time. Life is progress, so you should now know that you will constantly be working towards improvement. If we feel improvement and progress, that is when we can feel true joy.

Exercise

Section	Score	What makes it a 10?
Family	9	See them more often
Health and Fitness	8	Get my weight to below 65kg and work out daily with improving functional fitness
Fun	8	More fun nights required!
Spirituality	8	Meditate at least 3 times per week
Career/ Business	8	Own multiple companies
Finances	8	Have savings of $100,000, assets of more than $5m
Personal Development	9	Read more every night before sleeping

Your turn. (I have left the sections blank, as you need to name them and decide how to separate the categories.)

Section	Score	What makes it a 10?

Get a Mission Statement

Every company who is remotely serious about their business, has what is known as a mission statement. A mission statement describes the sole purpose and values of the company, the ideal and achieved vision that the founder had in mind when she started out. As you have completed several exercises in this book, you should by now have identified what is really important to you deep down. Several times you have been asked to write lists of what you want to achieve in your life. You have been asked to visualize what your life looks like, and I have suggested how to get yourself some life standards. So write a sentence or two that sums you up. Just worry about what sums you up today. Of course, you can and should change this over time. Mine would look something like this.

I want to help others find ways to make their lives the best that they can be, in the quickest and most fun way possible!

Exercise

Let's write your mission statement. If you're stuck, answer these questions:

1. What is important to you?
2. What do you want to achieve?
3. How do you want to do it?

Engage—Go Back to Your Childhood

Create your own Happiness, by taking full responsibility for each of your Actions

I hear you. Why do we need to go back to our childhoods? Because this is when our delicate little minds were programmed. Our childhood is when we learned and discovered how life works. This is when we were programmed with all the social rules and workings, and this is why we need to go back to this time and *re*-program the old noodle.

Think back to the age when you stopped asking questions. First you're born, and your parents or guardians do everything in their power (if you were lucky like me) to get you going, to get you eating, to get you moving, to get you talking, to get you crawling, then walking and speaking, then singing and dancing. Maybe they pushed you even further: music lessons, gymnastics, football and other sports, debate team, other languages—the list is endless. At the same time (bizarrely), parents spend a lot of effort getting you to stop doing things too. "SSsssshhh!" "Sit down, be quiet!" "Stop touching that!" "Get out of there!" "Stop picking your nose!" "Get your hand off your"—you get my point. When you asked "why" as a child over and over again, what happened? You were probably told to shush, to stop being annoying, to stop doing someone's head in. I know I was definitely told this, and I was very cute. I advise you to go back to your childhood. Ask why. Ask why not? Ask a lot.

Ask as much as possible. Get your childish and innate curiosity back. You might get your best answers and ideas by just simply improving the way things currently are. How did we get electricity? Because of that unhappy thought that the candle wasn't as bright as daylight, and how awesome would it be if lights were automatic? Simple, right?

Live your life with curiosity, joy, passion, and happiness. Find out what these things are for you, and you will quite literally and easily transform your life. Allow yourself to find the simple things in life that entertain you and make you happy. What do you remember as being joyful in your childhood? If you had a really shitty experience, think of today. If you didn't have a shitty experience, then close your eyes and transport yourself back to a time in your childhood when you were laughing and stress free. From my childhood, I remember bike rides in the summer. I would get on my peach colored racer called Chloe and off we would go, as a family, flying downhill, sometimes with hands and legs waving everywhere. I remember feeling invincible and carefree; I was definitely not stressed about everyday miniscule crap. The sun was shining, the sky was blue, the smell of cut grass tickled my nostrils. The air was swishing past my ears. Occasionally there were flies—once I'm pretty sure I swallowed one—but life was great! Everyone has these memories and moments, and everyone is capable of evoking these feelings.

Gratitude

Express joy, be grateful, and say happy thank yous for everything in your life. Be grateful today for what you have, and for what you might have tomorrow. When you praise, compliment, feel grateful and happy, you are operating on the closest level to your happiness, to your joy.

Exercise

Take a moment. Think back to a happy childhood memory. Feel yourself in your new little kid body, and see through your childhood eyes. What do you see? Who do you see? What do you hear? Who do you hear? How do you feel? What temperature is it? Linger in this feeling and make it stronger and stronger and stronger. Let this feeling of innocent and infinite possibility flush over your today body.

Defining: Know What You Mean and Mean What You Say

To achieve something, to achieve anything, you definitely need to know what that something is. A great place to start is defining the words. We are all so very different, and success to you will be very different from what success is to me. Success, as a very generic definition, means doing what you want for as long or short as you want to, that you love doing it, and that you are happy doing it.

Literally, having it all.

But the question is, what is *all* for you? For example, "I am working for myself and I no longer need to check my bank account. I will check it because I am so happy to see how much is in it. I am perfectly happy with my work and purpose and working on my own business and taking lots of fantastic trips around the world. I am enjoying my family to trips to visit me in Dubai, and I am planning huge, exciting things for next year!" If you were to write your own statement, it might look similar; some parts might be similar, or they might be nothing alike. Luckily, we are not all looking for the same things.

Exercise

Define the following words.

Success

Happiness

Having it all

Make a List

There is nothing more de-motivating than feeling like you're working away, plugging away, trucking on, or whatever you call it, and yet also feeling like nothing is happening. How you will want to track this depends entirely on your personality. As for me, I make lists. I either make a lists before I do things (a task list) or sometimes I prefer to write a list of the things at the end of the day (an achievements list). Either way, it invigorates my soul to see progress, and ticking things off is incredibly motivating for me. Personally, I am a list freak. I could actually have a list of all my lists. But they are really helpful, and I am incredibly organized and efficient because of them. Whether it's "Groceries" or "Ideas for my book," the lists helps me track my thoughts and I am able to go back in at any point to amend them, send them to myself, or delete them.

If you're not in love with my previous chapter about vision boards, or you just need some motivation and self-encouragement, try writing a "Santa List." Do you remember, as a child, when you would write the most elaborate gift list to Santa for Christmas? When we were kids, my sister and I used to sit for weeks before Christmas, pouring through all the catalogs we could get our little hands on. We would go through the pages selecting everything we thought we might ever possibly want. This is a great way to visualize. I still love going through magazines and cutting out pictures of homes, cars, and clothes I want. You know, it's funny. I really didn't think I had a particular clothing style until I sat down and cut out all the outfits I would love to have. When I did this, I had the most beautiful wardrobe collection, one that clearly has a very definite style, and now I know what that style is.

Ask yourself this today: what is it that you really want? You must know what you want. Goals, work, life, finances, love, or other things. Write up your Santa lists and read and lust after those things often. (Positively and with the possibility of it being real in your mind).

Goal Setting

Big Goals

I started writing this book and gave myself a deadline of two weeks to get the first draft done. I type fast. I have been obsessed with reading every self-help and motivational book I could get my hands on for years, and I knew that when I focused and sat down to write, it would just flow. It has taken several years of preparation to get myself to this point, but when you are ready to do it, you will know it, and you will need to take definite action. Don't be scared to set yourself hard targets. If it actually takes me two and a half weeks or even three weeks to write my first draft, will I be disappointed?

Absolutely not! I will be delighted!

Life Mapping

The most useful thing that I did in my early twenties was to map out the next five years of my life. Plan out everything, from your career progression to your personal relationships (this does not just mean partner; it also means your parents, siblings, and others). Decide what your health looks like, decide what your fitness level is, decide what you weigh. Decide how much money you earn, what type of car you drive, and in what kind of house you live. What does your partner do that you love? What qualities are really important to you? The list can go on and on.

If you struggle to set goals on your own, seriously consider getting yourself an executive coach. Coaches are trained to ask you the difficult questions that make you think, to make you process information, and to enable and bring you to point where you are able to have those aha moments. They help you to get your ideas down on paper and help you focus your ideas into an actionable to-do list. Good coaches will always have a coach for themselves.

Chunk it Down

Chunk down your huge, global domination plans and break them into bite size chunks that you can actually achieve.

Jodie, a teacher from Cambridge, England, came to a coaching session and had huge goals for every area in her life. She wanted to change her career, take a new course, start up a new business, lose ten pounds, start a new relationship, and start writing a course book. She was warm, funny, very ambitious, and had so many ideas running around her head, but so many ideas were disabling her and she was stuck. She couldn't see the forest for the trees, so to speak. In an hour and a half, we had prioritized each of these goals and decided to focus on working on the top two. These were changing her career and choosing a new educational course. By asking her questions about what was really, really important to her, she discovered what needed to be done, and we were able to create actionable goals for her to easily accomplish. For changing her career, she had a couple of ideas as to what she wanted to do, but nothing was concrete, and the more that she tried to be flexible and open to all ideas, the more she found herself stuck. So in asking her what she needed to help her decide, we came up with the following easily actionable goals. (I keep repeating the word *easily*, and this is important, because crappy coaches will try to force you to agree to do things that you probably know, deep down inside, you are never going to do. Actions should be easy, and you should leave your coaching session confident and energized to go and do it.)

- Research executive coaching online
- Research full-time teaching positions in London
- Research freelance teaching opportunities in London/ Cambridge
- Speak to Claire, a colleague who is a career counsellor
- Ask friend Rachel if she can be shadowed at work for a day to see if Jodie likes it

Jodie was comfortable with working on all of these points, and she skipped out of our session ready and willing. Two months later, I received a message from her, saying she had handed in her notice, had paid for her course, and was delighted with the clarity that only one session with me had given her. ☺

Feel it

There is absolutely no point in achieving any of your goals if you won't feel awesome when you have done so. So think about your goal, and right now allow yourself to feel that feeling you associate with the amazingness of having your goal, achieving your goal, and successfully getting what you want. Close your eyes and let the feeling of amazingness and success wash over your body, into your pores, and from your heart pump it out through all your veins, right to the tips of your fingers and toes.

Exercise

Let's take your big goal and create yummy bite-size goals for you to get your teeth stuck into. Nom, nom, nom!

Big Goal

Example: In six months I want to be married. (I hear this all the time when usually the person is single and hasn't met anyone he or she wants to marry.)

Okay, I do love a challenge, and usually through a coaching session the actionable goals for wanting to get married are usually something like this.

- Join a dating website or group or go somewhere you are likely to meet people you will be interested in.
- Ask trusted friends to set you up on dates.
- Have pre-set criteria for what your date should be like (and yet remain flexible to be swept off your feet by the unexpected).
- Create a vision board with your perfect marriage and wedding on it. (Make sure you hide this if you bring a date home—you know, to avoid looking like a psycho.)

All of these mini goals are easy, achievable, and most likely going to be a truckload of fun. If you are uncomfortable with internet dating, then don't do it. All of your tasks to achieve your goals should be things you actually want to do.

Go forth, chunk it down, and get achieving.

Commitment

Let me ask you this: what are the types of things that stop you from committing and achieving your dreams? Pop this into your mental microwave and get thinking as you read through this chapter. Ding!

What could potentially be stopping you from living your ideal life that your dreams are made of? Is it a belief that while it would be awesome and you would love it, that it's (in reality) a bit of a fairy tale that you might never really get your hands on? Is it the belief that, in order to achieve what you really want, you have to sacrifice everything you value and work twenty hours a day? (And perhaps, deep down, you don't really want to be bothered with those twenty-hour days.) Is it a feeling that you are alone and you don't really have the people to guide and support you? Or could it be that you just don't know where to get started?

Think about the beliefs that the people around you hold. Examine their attitudes and decide whether they are positive and energizing, or negative and draining. What did your parents tell you growing up? What do your friends believe? What opinions are they trying to convince you of? Do your magazines and television programs tell you what you want and what you should aspire to be like? Is it possible that these opinions floating around in your space might be affecting your beliefs and impacting and affecting your choices? Remember, these opinions are just that: some other person's opinions. What you are trying to gain here is a sense of objectivity. Without objectivity, you will never be able to make up your own mind and decide what is important to you.

What does the word *commitment* mean to you? Marriage? Dedication to a vision? A slightly unhealthy obsession with accumulating money? What is it you currently believe, and what is it that you need to believe? Commitment, for me, means knowing what I want and proactively embracing every possible opportunity that comes my way to get me there. It does not mean that I say yes to everything; I say no to the things that I dread, because that gut feeling is a guide to whether I am following the right path or not.

Commitment is also balance for me. I do not want to be obsessed. Commitment means working solidly and efficiently, and to work solidly and efficiently I know I need to have rest and relaxation too.

Are you prepared to commit to something right now? Yourself? To being the best you that you can be? I know that this sounds like pure cheese factory talking here, but today you have a choice: to be mediocre and live the best life that you justify to yourself is all you can have, or to commit right now to putting a bit of effort in, be amazing, and live the most amazing life you can think of. The choice belongs to you. I hope you choose well. ☺

Exercise Part 1

What is blocking you from committing to your goals?

Examples:

1. My full time job
2. My husband/wife thinks I'm mad and I should just stay in my job and earn a safe salary.
3. I don't have the money to get started.

Exercise Part 2

Turn your blocks into steps or actions.

1. My job is currently keeping my bills and life on track. I still have five evenings and two full days to do whatever I choose.
2. I need to educate my partner and really explain how important this is to me, and how much I really need his or her support.
3. I will easily find someone to partner with, or an investor who wants to achieve the same things I do.

Eliminate Distractions

I don't have enough time to do what I really want to do. Heard this one? Yes, I might even have said it myself… many, many times. I love social media, my phone, and honestly, even thought I have massively reduced TV time, still there is too much Netflix. But if we worked out how much time we actually spend on these things, we would see how much potential time we have. The people I hear saying "I don't have time" the most are in fact the people who never lift their heads from their phones. Imagine if you just became one degree less available? Would it completely destroy your life? (NB, if the answer is yes to this question, you need to go back and do the wheel of life again, because something is *not* right here!) In order to achieve something, we must focus on it, and focusing will require a tiny bit of time. Find the courage to switch these wonderful inventions off and spend quality time working towards your dreams.

> *A poor man has a big television, but a rich man has a big library.*

Distractions can also be another word for procrastination, or the Big E: Excuses. We can spend our whole day making excuses. I didn't get up this morning to exercise because I was tired and couldn't trail my big butt out of bed. I didn't work on my business plan today because I wanted to catch up on the gossip with the girls instead. I didn't talk to my manager, as I wanted to today, because I didn't plan my day properly and was busy over my lunch break. I didn't get all of my work done today because I just couldn't peel myself off Facebook. Are any of these ringing a bell? If not, write your own here. I didn't _____

_____ because I was _____

_____.

In order to overcome this, you need your reason to do it to be stronger than these crappy excuses. These excuses are weak, but we accept them because they justify why we didn't do something. They pacify us, like a baby and his dummy. Stop pacifying! Stop excusing and stop allowing the distractions.

You want to be a millionaire? Will you become a millionaire by watching *Who Wants to be a Millionaire?* Don't think so! Switch it off and get on the road to your Amazing life.

Exercise

In order to eliminate distractions, you need to identify them, so here we go.

Number	Stop Distracting Me!
Example	My colleagues are forcing me to go for after-work drinks too often!
1	
2	
3	
4	
5	

Task

Now we can plan our tool to help us in these situation. Together, let's choose one of these distractions and work out a way to eliminate it. If your distraction is work drinks with colleagues, plan your excuse to get away early, and write it down now so you are prepared and not caught off-guard. Also, think about what you are going to do with that extra time so you are motivated to give up the drinks. What will you do? What will you achieve? How will you feel when you achieve it? Write this down so you can see how managing your distractions properly can affect and enhance the potential of your life.

Exercise

Distraction	outcome	Feeling	Solution	outcome	Feeling
example My Colleagues are forcing me to go for after-work drinks too often!	I lose an evening and feel crap at work the next day	☹	Tell them I planned to meet an old school friend	I have a free evening to start my business plan	☺
1					
2					
3					
4					
5					

Repetition: The Key to Your Success

Repetition means get into the habit of routinely doing something.

Repetition is the number 1 most crucial key to your impending and awesome success. By setting up repetition, and I mean, routines - you will create a system for success. If you stick to the routine for long enough, this routine will become an ingrained habit, and *your* habits are the key to *your* success. When you find anything that works for you, keep doing it. Rereading your list of goals and priorities will help get them embedded into your mind, and don't forget: your mind will automatically find ways for this to happen, like magic. I advise that you just start in any small way that you can; just change one habit and commit to doing something once. Do you like it and want to do it again, and feel better for having done it? If yes, plan it again for another time. Go on, plan it in, to do it one more time, and take it from there. So let me recap this for you: creating your habit essentially creates your routine, and it is routine that will *ensure* your success. You can clearly see what people's routines are. A person who goes to the gym daily looks completely different from a person who has been once in the past three weeks. When you establish a routine, you will absolutely see the difference in your life. You will see it. You will feel it. You will reap the reward from it and you will love it. You just have to remain strategic enough in your mind, to know that this will happen without you seeing the result on day 1.

Good habits will lead you to success and bad habits will lead you to...that's right, whatever bad habit you might have yourself. I love a glass of wine, but unfortunately it doesn't love me. When I overindulge, this seemingly harmless habit leads to me not going to the gym, which leads to me not getting up early in the morning, which leads to not having my productive mornings, not getting work done, and therefore not being a millionaire. LOL! This might seem slightly melodramatic perhaps, but all of my actions have consequences, and I take 100 percent responsibility for myself, my actions, and my outcomes.

A good habit to get into is talking to yourself. And I don't mean out loud, while staring at someone, with your tongue hanging out, and drooling. However, you should get into the habit of reevaluating how you are feeling about your life and keep yourself in your own communication loop. Constantly ask yourself, "Is that what I really, *really*, REALLY want to be doing?" Your feelings are your main indicator as to whether or not you're on the right track. For me, right now, I can't stop writing. I want to share what has helped me, I want to create a community that is sharing and talking, and I want to get this book written so I can do that. When I am doing anything else, all I can think about is what I could be doing to help this book get finished. Are you following your passion? Are you following what makes you happy? Are you following that little all-knowing tug that you get in your tummy?

If you're naturally a lazy person, don't panic—there are ways you can still create habits for success. Use technology and set up reminders. Set reminders that are realistic and for things you will enjoy doing because then you won't mind.

All of these techniques and tips need constant work. I frequently read motivational literature, listen to podcasts, watch motivators on YouTube, and research the products they create to remind and enhance myself constantly. As I'm watching them, I'm thinking to myself that I know this stuff, but it's difficult to always keep it up. The constant reminder will make you absorb it and become it.

As humans, we need repetition. Whether we admit it or not, we have habits, good or bad, from getting your daily Starbucks latte to promising to go out and always cancelling at the last minute; from putting off work until the deadline is chasing you and biting you on your ass to constantly saying yes and trying to please everyone. Quite simply, you could replace shitty habits with better ones. If you need to shift a few pounds, replace your daily latte with an Americano with milk—and walk there, don't order for delivery.

The small changes really do clock up and get you better results than you're getting today. Fact.

Here's a fact: you cannot succeed at what you're *not* doing. Research shows it takes forty days to break an old habit and create a new one, so we need to break it down one day at a time. Just start with something small, commit to it once, and see how it feels. If you feel good and positive, then plan to do it again. All of these next times will add up to forty, and by the time you get there you will have formed a routine and a formula for success. Get the ball rolling and soon you will be running behind it trying to keep up.

Exercise

Put repetition into practice. Organize yourself. If you have a phone, then you have the technology already. Use your phone and plan in the tasks you like. Whether it is me time, affirmations, or lists, plan it in and remind yourself to do it until you have retrained your brain and you act automatically.

Resilience

The time to stand up is when you think you cannot do it again.
This is when Breakthroughs happen.

Making changes in your life is like a diet. How funny is it that people eat with terrible habits for thirty years, and then cannot believe that they can't lose all the weight they need to in two weeks? If you expect to make a few changes and have your life change immediately, I hope you're right. I hope you can and do see change. For others, it may take longer, and you must be like the resilient salesperson. You must convince yourself that you need to keep going, that you are the original Duracell bunny. It is only with routine and repetition that you will get there. If you fold at your first failing experience, then you have failed. We need to mentally change the word *failure* into *progress*. If you are failing, you are progressing and learning, and therefore are moving forward. If you continue to keep going and going, you will get there. The fastest way to success is to increase your failure rate. It just depends on how much work and experience and courage you are prepared to show to get there. Quite often, it is through a rough life experience that we find out what we are made of. Do you stay in bed and give up, or do you choose to get up and soldier on?

Jim Rohn gives the example of a baby: he's trying to walk, and he gets up and falls over, gets up and falls over while trying to get up, and gets up and falls over, and again and again. At what point does he stop trying? Does it even cross his mind to stop trying? No! He gets tired and what does he do? He takes a break, he has a nap, and then he starts trying all over again. Another point is the people around him. Do they stop championing him? Do they stop supporting? Do they say, "Perhaps you shouldn't do this darling, it's a bit risky." No. Of course we do not.

Resilience is a sort of determination, a confidence that you know you are doing the best thing for you. You should have this confidence. You are the expert in you, you are the expert of your life, and there is no one who can tell you better than you. I do not mean you should reject all advice ever given to you. But I do mean that you need to evaluate the advice and decide if it's right for you to take it or not. Get confident in your desires and standards and you will automatically build your level of resilience.

Rejecting Rejection

Maybe you already know the story of Colonel Sanders, if not, it is the story of a man who knew he had something; who did sales pitch after sales pitch, getting nos everywhere he went. Maybe it was his sales pitch, maybe it was his approach, maybe his appearance, or maybe his luck that day, but after 1,000 tries, he eventually got that yes. And major respect to the Colonel for never giving up.

Twelve publishers rejected *Harry Potter* by J.K. Rowling. We know they're all kicking themselves now.

There are a million cheesy stories like this, and if you don't feel remotely inspired or energized by them, then recheck your pulse, because there's something wrong with you. However, not everyone has the stamina or the balls to be rejected 1,000 times and keep going. It's tough when everyone around you is telling you "you're mad," "give up," "get a job," "grow up" or whatever it is they are saying.

Rejecting rejection is a skill. And quite frankly, it's important not to confuse it with being an arrogant ass. I'm not encouraging you to become an unfeeling, bouncy wall that everything bounces off of. Rejecting rejection is a skill that comes from preparation, and anyone can do this.

Any good salesperson will tell you that success in sales is simply a numbers game. Being a salesperson in this environment makes you resilient, and a little bit allergic to people saying no to you. Any awesome salesperson will tell you that the best sale is one that is referred to you already (that is, someone else has done the donkey work for you), or one that is so easy because you researched the person and situation beforehand. Either way, there is a simple combination here: Preparation + Opportunity = Success. The easier route is to go around batting off the nos like you are swatting flies. You will probably be stressed out and exhausted. The smart and efficient way is to do your homework. It will prepare you for the nos and put you in exactly the right place for when someone is going to say yes to you.

So now, we intellectuals who have absorbed my message of efficiency over quantity have minimized the nos. But it will still hurt when you get them, so prepare for this situation.

Imagine all the objections someone will give you and prepare your answers.

Prepare a response for when someone says no. Realize it's his or her choice, and that doing this perhaps doesn't take that person towards his or her vision. Be gracious and grateful for that person's time. It might not be for that person today, but something might happen tomorrow, and he or she could call you back.

Ask the person if he or she knows anyone who might be interested. Getting a referral for someone else will give you a great head start towards that yes.

The Secret and the
Law of Attraction

The Secret is a book which has also been made into a movie. The concept of the book is motivational, and it explains the theory of the Law of Attraction. If you can't get your hands on the book, you must watch the movie. *The Secret* begins with Bob Proctor explaining the Law of Attraction. He explains that what you think about is exactly what you bring about in your life. What's inside your mind will become your external reality. If you can see it in your mind, you will hold it in your hand. Another motivator who appears in *The Secret*, Mike Dooley has built an entire business around the concept that "thoughts become things." The world is based on this law, and it is always present in the same way that gravity never switches off. Whether we understand it or believe it, it is there and it is happening.

This book had a huge influence on me and my life. Before reading this book, I definitely liked to think that I was sharp, sarcastic, and shrewd. Now, I actually care much less about what people think of me. I hope they think I'm lovely, of course, but I spend my time proactively trying to be a great person who lives to their values and encouraging and helping greatness from those around me, all in a positive way because I really believe that this positivity and loveliness will come back to me tenfold.

Affirmations to Declarations

It's the repetition of affirmations that leads to belief.

If we are what we eat, then we are what we read, we are what we think, and we definitely are what we say we are. Affirmations are a good way to change your thought process, as what you say out loud again and again begins to sound right. Pick something you want to develop or work on—your confidence, your job, your weight, or your finances—and force yourself, first thing in the morning when you're brushing your teeth or peeing, to tell yourself how amazing you are at it. "I am sexy, I am slim!" Make yourself shout it louder and louder, get your body involved and swinging. "I am sexy! I got my promotion! I have savings! I am fit!" Initially you will feel like a total muppet, but embrace the feeling of being a dick, and persist. This action will give you positive energy, and you will even feel sexier and more slim, or like you have already gotten that promotion.

No, lazy buns, it is *not* enough to think this inside your head. The whole point of this is to externalize and change our feelings. Our bodies and minds are connected, and we can and need to use our bodies to break through to our minds. Follow my lead: say out loud, "Yes I can!" Now get off your seat—come on, move your ass for one second, get up out of your seat, punch your fist into the air, and shout, "Yes I can!" Feel the difference. Feel your heartbeat increase. Feel your energy level increase. Now you decide which person you want to be like: the ass sitting in the chair speaking the words, or the engaged, motivated, energetic person who took action and got up and punched the air. If you're currently in a coffee shop, feel free to do this later, unless you have balls of steel—in which case, I salute you.

Total Time: Thirty seconds per day.

The point? Action creates energy and momentum.

Exercise

Find the affirmations that you need to say. As I said previously, embrace the dickheadness of it all and say it loud and proud.

Number	Shout it out!
Example	I am confident, I am successful, I feel great!
1	
2	
3	
4	
5	

Task

Fill in this exercise immediately; do *not* leave it to later! You know your needs already. Trust your instincts and write. Start your affirmations today. Just do it!

Here's a variation of what I say to myself in the mirror in the morning—that's right, while I'm brushing my teeth, and doing whatever else I do in the morning.

I love my life, I love my apartment, I love my view, I love my car, I love my bathroom, I love my son, I love my sister, I love my parents, I love my whole family, I love my job, I love my salary and my financial freedom, I love my hair, I love my eyes, I love my legs, I love my life!

And repeat!

Focus On What You Are Great At

I remember being in high school and struggling with mathematics and French. My parents did what all amazing parents would do and paid a fortune (I'm sure) for tutors to get me through my GCSEs (General Certificate of Secondary Education). Am I grateful? Absolutely. (My parents are awesome.) This was the logical thing to do, and I was glad to get all my GCSEs and move on to A Levels, and so on. However, what happened was I ended up getting a better grade in A Level French, a subject I hated by the way, and got a lower mark in A Level Music, which I loved and was actually pretty good at. Does this make sense? I don't think so.

All too often, we spend time focused on what we are not really good at, we make sure we are developing our weakest areas, but what happens then is we are neglecting our gifts — and these gifts are what we really need to focus on, to improve, and to enhance. As humans, we are all different and individual. Do we really need a race of people who are all mediocre at everything? No way! Focus on what you are good at and outsource what you are not. In business and in life, you will be happier.

Focus as well on what matters to you. Do not bounce from thing to thing your whole life or you will get old and feel totally shaken, not stirred. Focus on the top three things that matter to you the most, or that need the most attention in order to be living your best life ever.

Exercise

As before, in order to know what we are good at, we must take a moment to think about and write a list of our skills.

Number	I am awesome at...
Example	I am a great communicator!
1	
2	
3	
4	
5	

Here are some questions to help you identify your skills.

- What do you *love* doing?
- What makes you laugh the loudest?
- What are you doing when you want to do extra? When you don't want to stop?
- What inspires you to do more?
- What makes you feel thankful for your life?
- What makes you *curious* to know more?

Task

How can you improve something you are already good at? Is there a class you could take, or a group you could join? Brainstorm ideas to take your skills to a whole new level.

Originality

Just be you. You will automatically be original. This is the key, and the truest way to be original is to just be the best version of you that you can be. We are all unique, right? We are all different, have different values and motivations, different hopes and aspirations. So if you want to be original, stick with what you know best: you. As you start visualizing how you want your life to be, your mind will be producing ideas at a rate that you will hardly be able to keep up with. Use this, explore and this search will lead you to the one thing that is original — originally yours. How do you be original? It will come with time, but you must start with unoriginal first. An idea can become the most contagious thing if you are brave enough to say it out loud and brainstorm further ideas. You will find yourself ending up in a very different place from where you started. What you thought was an insignificant passing of inspiration could turn into your future life.

Opportunity

Train yourself to see the opportunity in everything. This takes time and focused practice. See solutions. Make yourself see solutions because they exist, they are there, people are seeing them every day, and if you see the right solution at the right time, you will find your purpose and happiness in life. The door only closes when you say it closes. And when you choose that the door has closed, you still have options. Turn around and see the gorgeous big windows opening out onto the beach. See the potential where others cannot. See that in life there are in fact many ways to do anything. Anywhere you want to go, there are several options for your route.

With any course you want to study, there will be choices in course type, tutor, and venue. For any product you want to launch, there will be several ways to do it, and you will get to choose which one you are most comfortable with. This must sound quite high on the cheesy factor, but think of a time when something crap happened and you thought you couldn't bounce back: you split up with someone who you thought was special, lost someone close to you or didn't get the job/pay raise you were hoping for. Whatever it was, look at how you dealt with it. Did you move on? Did you get out of bed the next day? Was it as bad as you thought? Has something crap happened and it actually turned out to be the best thing that ever could have happened? Did you get a better job? A better partner? This happens quite often in this weird and wonderful life. Force yourself to see any sort of blessing in something bad and you will easily survive it.

@HowtoLiveAmazingLife
facebook.com/LiveAmazingLife

Financially

How your parents view money can affect you too. Growing up, I remember my dad's favorite phrase was, "Do you think money grows on trees?" Or another good one was "Who do you think I am, Rockefeller?" Or if something was expensive, he would say loudly in the shop, "And you're not even wearing a mask!" (that is, they were robbing him). We (my mum, sister, and I) were always mortified but laughing. What my dad really meant was, "No, you can't have it, because money is difficult to come by and it shouldn't be wasted on nonessentials." This was a completely reasonable perception. Until very recently in my life, I thought it would be incredibly difficult or impossible to make a lot of money. And therefore, until very recently in my life, I found it incredibly difficult and impossible to make a lot of money. But how wrong I was. When you are grateful, visualize, and follow your passion, follow your joy, follow what makes you happyand repurpose your steps,—the money can just flow into you.

Exercise

It is up to you whether you need to do this exercise or not, although I would advise you to try it even if you think you have no issues. You just never know what will come about. Let's work out sayings that you remember family members using when you were a child, and let's create new sayings to reprogram your mind.

Statements I remember

"Money doesn't grow on trees" changes to "Money flows easily and frequently."

"She is so quiet" changes to "She is so confident, and a brilliant orator!"

Now your turn.

Statements you remember

1. _____. becomes

_____

2. _____becomes

._____

3. _____. becomes

._____.

Responsibility

There is you, and then there is you…and, oh yeah, there is you. Perhaps you have people in your life you can depend on, and if you do, please be grateful for them and look after them. Appreciate them, love them, and thank them. If you do not think you have dependable people in your life, well, reconsider, because actually you do. You have you. You control your life, your destiny, how you approach situations; there is only you. The sooner you get this into your head the better. The sooner you take control and take yourself by the balls and have a good conversation with yourself, the better your life will be for it. If your life is not how you want it to be, I'm sorry to be the bitch to tell you this, but it's actually your fault and only you can change it. Really, I'm sorry if this comes as a smack in the face, but the way your life is today reflects how you have acted in the past and the decisions you have made. The amazing news is that you are able to change this right now, today. By readjusting your mindset, by improving how you respond to situations and choices, you can change and affect and improve your life immensely. This may seem like a big project, but break it down, start with something small, and repeat. Create the habits you want and watch in awe as your life transforms.

Have you have ever blamed something else for something you have done? (And if you're shaking your head, horrified, I might call you a fraud.) We have all done this. We have all blamed someone else or some other circumstances as reasons why we have made a poor choice, when in reality only we were responsible, and the fault could only lie with us.

When you do accept this fact, things can change quickly. As 2022 was coming in, I was so excited. I would say, "2022 is going to be my year!" I would finish my book, and create a course range that would be sold online. I had huge plans, and I needed January to be very productive. My family was staying over Christmas and didn't leave until the fifth of January. I decided I could really do with a couple of days of chillaxing. Then I was struck down by the superbug death plague (that was really just a flu bug.) Ten days later, I scraped myself back to work and wasn't 100 percent feeling normal for another four or five days. Then I had to catch up on my networking and social engagements, and before I knew it I was going to bed on 31 January, devastated that I hadn't achieved any of the goals I had set for myself in January. I was one month behind. I felt miserable. I felt totally crap. I felt like this would have a knock-out effect on the rest of my year. In my mind, I had not finished my book because of this and I had completely ruined my 2022. So, what did I do? I acknowledged that January was not as I had hoped. I convinced myself that my body needed that time to heal and get over the flu bug. I went to bed on 31 January resolved that my 2022 would start over on the first of February; I would awaken refreshed and energized and ready to get started again. And I did. February was awesome. I got a mini book finished, a product ready for Amazon, and the majority of this book completed. ☺ I made a decision, and I changed my mind, and my life, in five minutes.

Exercise

Repeat this affirmation:

I have the control, I have the power, I am amazing! I HAVE the control, I HAVE the power, I AM amazing! I HAVE THE CONTROL, I HAVE THE POWER, I AM AMAZING!

Let Go of the Past

We can't do anything about what happened yesterday; we can only affect today and tomorrow, from our actions today. (KB)

If it was shit, get over it. Shit happens, and I'm sorry it had to happen to you. But *only* you can decide how traumatized your have been by your experience and how much you need to wallow in your feelings, or to acknowledge and deal with it, then put that away into a box and into your past. Do not allow or give permission to something in your past that was shit now control your present and affect your future. Deal with the shit properly; grieve, and do whatever you need to do to move on. If it takes a year, look at this as an investment in your future rather than a waste; it is an investment in your future to allow yourself to deal with things properly, to free yourself to be able to get your groove on and live your most amazing life possible.

You should also decide that you may need to disregard things or opinions or "facts" that you were told as a child. Quite often, parents and teachers project things onto children that are productive for them at the time (that is, to help create a peaceful environment), but that may affect how you operate and perceive things later in life. If you were told as a child that you were so shy, so quiet, so good, you began to associate being shy with being good. I know I did. Everyone—my parents and even their friends— used to say it. I remember being allowed to sit with my mum and her friends as they chatted because I was so mature, but what they really meant was that I was quiet enough to not annoy them. I used to find out lots of gossip that way. However, was I eternally shy? No! University and working as a waitress in a bar sorted that out. Now, I have actually developed my social skills and I am on the other end of the scale of talkativity. When I tell people today that I didn't speak until I was sixteen years of age, they don't believe me.

Positive Mindset—How to Get it

How to be happy—the big question, huh? The mother of all questions, and yet only you have the answer. Not me. Thanks for reading and good night. No, seriously, I'm still here, but it's true: only you can tell you what makes you happy. You have standards or rules in your life, and when any one of these is broken it will make you unhappy. Maybe only big things make you happy? Maybe you're asking, "When was the last time I was truly happy?" I can tell you my answer: five minutes ago, when my lovely friend made me a cup of coffee. I'm grateful and happy for all of the small things and privileges that I get to experience. I do not have to wait to win the lottery before I allow myself to be happy and feel happiness. Before I leave work I always write down a list of achievements from that day. This helps me realize the value I added and eliminates thoughts of *I'm not doing a good enough job*. I realize I do not need to bring in a huge sale or launch a new marketing initiative. The value I added could be that I got an awesome new contact, or that I trained someone to do something new. These are steps towards a bigger success, and I will congratulate myself every chance I get.

Be a winner! Be a champion! You are what you say you are, so decide it and say it. Say it loud and say it proud, party people! Stand out from the crowd—that crowd of unfortunate individuals who think it is intellectual to make snide remarks and sarcastic comments. But quite frankly, that is truly bullshit. Stand out and apart from these people. Today, I make a point of staying clear of these people, as they are dangerous to my own mindset, and therefore to my own happiness and success. Be the best you that you can be, and do *not* accept anything less from yourself or those around you.

The glass is always full. You think it's empty? Give up your possessions, live a few nights on the streets, and then think back to the lovely life you just left. Still empty? Imagine you have just been told your health is so bad that you literally only have a day or so left. Still empty? Don't be a muppet. You had the money to buy this book, and if you didn't have the money you somehow had the resources to get it. Therefore, your glass is full. Stoically, your glass is, in fact, whatever you say it is. If there are surrounding muppets telling you your glass is empty, limit the time you spend with them. They have limited vision and beliefs, and are people you should minimize your time with.

As a race of people, we are actually quite humble. There are a few exceptions, but most people do not sell themselves well.

In the book *Flip It: How to Get The Best Out of Everything* by Michael Heppell, he talks about a very useful technique to use when something negative happens. Try swapping the voice in your head that says "Why me?" with a voice that says "How can I improve this?" This is a vital skill to learn, as we have all wasted time and energy asking God or the world "Why has this happened to me?" when we should have been allowing ourselves to receive this negative situation as feedback, and taken responsibility for the things we could actually change.

Omitting the negative can help also. For example, you go on holidays and have some great experiences, but all of your flights get delayed. If you're omitting the negative, what should you tell people? Exactly! You tell them all about those wonderful experiences, with all their glorious details. Forget about the flights and be grateful and happy that you got home safely.

Planning

If you are happy with lists, then you may be comfortable taking them one step further into an action plan. I have a one-year plan, a five-year plan, a ten-year plan, and a life plan. These are not set in stone, but rather written on paper and always subject to reevaluation, modification, or total deletion. Now really, if you're saying that this is excessive, please know that all of my plans are flexible. I am able to improvise or change my plan entirely, but it is sssoooooooooo important to know where you want to go. If you want to wing it, then be happy to let someone else control how far you can get in life. If, on the other hand, you are like me and want the only person in life who restricts you to be you, then accept the power of responsibility, and take it like a champ. Planners are winners. Fact.

Exercise

Write a list of lists that you would like to write. Yes, seriously.

Number	List I need to write
Example	Write my bucket list of things I MUST do before I die
1	
2	
3	
4	
5	

Task

Complete one of these lists as soon as possible. Check your schedule; when can you realistically get twenty minutes to do this?

As soon as you know what you want, you can go get it.

The Circle of Trust

Select with a degree of caution the people you surround yourself with. We all have those friends whose names flash up on our mobiles and our stomachs fill with dread at answering the call, afraid of getting involved in a life sucking conversation. It is time to take small but precise action. It is time to make yourself a little bit less available to those energy vampires. It is time to find people who want to achieve the same things as you. With social media and social networking sites, this has become as easy as a click. (Exercise your own common sense. Don't go to meet anyone for the first time without someone you trust knowing where you are going. Don't meet anyone you don't know in a private place, and don't take sweets from strangers.) This is your time to increase your internal energy by surrounding yourself externally with like-minded people who care about the same things and share the same values and motives. If you tolerate crap, in life or from people, you will end up with crap. Instead, have high standards. Say no. You are the most important person in your life, and you matter. Anyone who tells you that you don't definitely shouldn't matter to you.

On the other side of the coin, there are great, awesome, positive, encouraging people whom you should proactively be spending more time with. Identify who these people are (and if you don't have any, find places where you might meet these people) and work out how you can develop your relationships with these elevating personalities.

Task

You need to identify your friends who support you and help build you up, and compare them to the friends who are energy vampires and try to break you down (even unwittingly). Once you have done this, you can proactively reduce the time spent with energy vampires and increase the time spent with those who will help you get to where you want to be.

Exercise

Here, we are going to focus on the positive. Let's focus on the friends who you find to be inspiring, supportive, active, genuine, and true friends. If you focus on these people and work out how to build your relationships with them, the others will naturally fall away so you don't have to actively lose them.

Positive Friend's Name	The attributes you admire in that person
1	
2	
3	
4	
5	
6	

Share

As humans, we are meant to connect; we are meant to share life and experiences and laughter with each other. Do not be precious about your ideas; do not be worried someone will steal them. There is enough abundance in the world for several people to have your idea and for all to do well from it. Besides, no one will ever do it exactly as you do. Sharing is caring, as my mum used to tell me, and if someone is such a lowlife that he or she would steal your idea, then bonus: you found this out and can separate yourself from that person immediately. Think of yourself as super lucky you found out, then ditch and move on. Never feel upset, because if your mind is working and you are reading, learning, and developing, you will explore and you will find something else.

It is also important to give back. There are so many benefits to giving back. Selfishly, there is the feel-good factor, and unselfishly, there is the fact that you are helping other people who could really use your help. Find something that you would love to be involved in; there are many groups and organizations, or you could even start your own.

Superheroes

Boring people call them mentors. In fact, people who want you to pay them to be your mentor call themselves mentors. I prefer the supercool term of Superhero! Whatever you want to call them, it is absolutely essential that you surround yourself and fill your life with these motivating superpeople, who do what you eventually want to be doing or have come from where you have come from and have achieved more than you think you can. Of course, it is absolutely possible to make changes to your life totally by yourself; it's just harder. However, it takes time to change behaviors, and if you seek support, you have a greater chance of being successful. Successful people naturally measure their performance and reevaluate their next move. You will learn this from them. Find people whom you admire, people whose books excite you when you read them. All of these superheroes are so much more accessible now thanks to social media and celebrity. Link with them on Twitter and Facebook, and watch as you are able to interact with them. Of course, the big ones will have people operating their social media, but do you think even a superhero wouldn't want an ego boost now and again, and read it for himself or herself? I bet you that person does.

Find the people you need to take you to the next level. Who are they and what do they do? Search social media; the internet is making this so easy for us now. Research and make your introduction.

Through school, we had teachers, but isn't it weird that we apparently stopped needing a teacher at sixteen, or eighteen, or twenty-one, or whatever time you left academia? If you need to get fit, the quickest way is with a personal trainer. If you need to lose weight, the quickest way is with some sort of support group, virtual or not. If you want to learn a language, the fastest way is with mentors who are nationals of the country where the language is spoken. Are you getting the picture? Having a mentor creates action. Where does the action come from? If you have to account for your actions, chances are you will be more successful than without having to.

If you want to do something or be something, ask someone who is already living your dream to help you, guide you, or teach you. Don't be worried about asking successful people for help. Keep in mind that the fastest way for you to really learn and know your profession is to teach it to someone else.

Most successful people love to share their knowledge, as working with others actually gives them a lot of ideas and inspiration. Successful people continually look for opportunities like these.

Don't waste your time asking your friends and family what they think unless they are qualified and successful in what you want to do. Quite often, family and friends think they are advising you from the right place—a place of security and comfort—but only you know deep down what you want and what feels right. Do not be swayed. Go and find the person who can actually help you.

Taking a Chance

We are scared of failure, scared of embarrassment, scared of the shame that comes with having made a mistake, or having judged something wrong. Who cares? Stop caring about failure. Life is an experience, and to get the right idea, you may have to go through several wrong ones. Accept this as part of the learning process and you will succeed. Would you rather go through the embarrassment of failing a few times to get the reward that you really want, or not try at all? I know what I'm doing. See you at the finish line, kiddos.

The Power of Now

The question might really be: why not now? What is stopping you from doing it? You now know what you want, you have your list of things to do, things to see, things you want. What exactly is preventing you from doing, seeing, and getting? You're thinking about it now, you are in the zone right now, so do something about it now. Don't wait. When you feel the urge, when you feel the instinct, when you feel the tiniest bit of energy, do something. Start and the ball will roll.

What might be stopping you from doing it today? I know you're busy. We are all busy. Ask yourself how much you want it. Give it a number out of ten. When you have identified what you want and how much you want it, then you suddenly find the motivation to get your butt in gear and get it started. You will find that starting is the hardest part; as soon as you start, the ball will start rolling and you will find yourself running after the ball trying to keep up.

Bodybuilders say the hardest lift is the butt lift off the sofa.

You will also find the universe moves things around to encourage you. But starting is your indication to the universe that this is what you want. Only then do you get the help you need—the space you need—and you will randomly meet people who will be useful to you.

What's the worst that can happen? You start and you don't like it, so you stop. Time wasted? Definitely not. You start and it doesn't work out very well. Time wasted? No, all experience is useful. You never start and someday you regret it. Time wasted? Definitely. Get on it.

Action—Just Start

There are two main ingredients to success: your passion, and a little momentum. Or, as Marshall Goldsmith describes in his book *Mojo: Direction and Speed*, "We have worked together on goal setting and identifying what makes you happy—what you really want and *need* to achieve. The second thing you now need to work on is creating momentum, and to do that you need to do just one thing: Start."

Two years ago, I had these crazy, huge ambitions (that secretly and very deep down I probably thought wouldn't happen). I wanted desperately to write a book that would help a person live his or her best life, and also to create an entire product range that I could sell through a website. What a huge, intimidating plan. I could have just looked at this plan and thought it was never going to happen, but instead I decided I just needed to get started. So for the book, I just started writing. I didn't start writing a book. I didn't start writing a chapter or a page. I started with one single word: *Amazing*.

Our minds will naturally find a million reasons not to do something. "It's too much effort." "I'm not a writer." "What if no one likes it?" Well here is where a sense of realism will help you. I already know that I can't please everyone. I already know that not everyone will like my book or theories. What do I do with that information? It doesn't really matter, because I don't care about those people. I am interested in helping people who want to be helped, and it is this that spurs me on.

As soon as I made a decision to do this properly and I started telling great people what I wanted to achieve, all I received was help and encouragement. To recap: the first step of my huge, daunting, and impossible project was one word on one page. It is that easy and it is that possible. (It also doesn't hurt that every time I meet any of my friends they ask me how it's going.)

Second, let's not confuse motion with action. You may be busy, but are you busy doing the right stuff? If you are busy doing a lot of the wrong stuff, you definitely won't arrive where you want to go. So how can you start? Decided and focused action. To create action, you are required to make decisions. I wanted to write a book, so I broke this down to the starting point: I would need to put some words on a page. If you want to start a business, perhaps your starting point is finding out what that process is. If you want to get married, do you have a partner yet? Find the fastest way to make a start and, as Nike tells us, "Just Do It."

Task

Pick a goal that you want to achieve. Think of a few small actions that could get you there and put them into a list so you know how to start. How will you feel once you have done it?

Exercise

Goal: To write a published book
1   Put some words on a page
2   Research how to get published
3   Speak to someone who has done this before

Your turn.

Goal:
1
2
3

Conclusion

Your life is about you, and you are important. Am I right? Your life will be as successful as you allow it to be. Attitude is a little thing that makes a *huge* difference. Your attitude will be contagious to those around you. The question is: is yours worth catching? ;)

Do whatever makes you happy, and do it proudly. I have been known to put on a sexy pair of high heels while writing this book in my pajamas, just to change my posture and my mood.

I really hope this book has made you think differently, even if it's only to say to yourself that change can actually be easy. If you have read the book properly, engaged with me, and completed the exercises, I hope you are pleased with the thoughts that have been provoked and that you are ready for change and greatness. I have genuinely written this book in order to give something to you. So if you register at my website www.howtoliveanamazinglife.com, I will continue to send you thoughts and new chapters and writings as I have them.

Take care peeps, look after yourselves and please keep in touch with me.

Lots of love,

Karen xoxo

So What's Next?

Work With Karen Directly

Sessions can be scheduled and held online or in person. Email us for more details: Karen@howtoliveanamazinglife.com.

Online Coaching Program

I have created a coaching program which still allows you direct access to me. It is a more beautifully affordable way to get coaching and help you achieve whatever it is you want to.

Check www.howtoliveanamazinglife.com for further details.

@liveamazinglife

Sort Your Life out TODAY!

If you cannot take one more single day where you feel like you are not in control, you are not living the life that you deserve. You are not living the life you are capable of if you are not getting what you want professionally. If you are not experiencing the depth of the relationships you want, then pick up this book now!

Coach, motivator, and author Karen Beggs will take you through the process and steps of what to actually do to bring your life back into track and ensure that you are experiencing the best and most amazing life that you can.

Coach and published author, Karen lives her most amazing life now in Dubai with her family. Having founded and invested in more than five companies, she continues to run a business and consult on organizational projects.

Karen Beggs

Printed in the United States
by Baker & Taylor Publisher Services